Of Light and Heat

I.
Across the sea
He dreams in riddles
When on respite from the sleepless nights
That move his lips
To longing.

II.
My love for you
Is a child's
Love of standing
In the eye of a storm
Knowing the cost.
It is loud and
Automatic and
A gravity unto itself.

My betrayal is
A child's, too.
Standing in this
Fascinating, beautiful
Chaos,
I am a casualty of
Its recklessness.

III.
I am assaulted that night
By flames that create
Shadows massive enough to obscure me
From heaven.

Tears like holy water
Essay to soothe my skin from the lashes
Of wicked tongues that
Recite my sin.
I pray for heaven
But fail to change.

Holy Spirit,
set me ablaze
With light,
Not heat.

<u>A Glimpse Into the Future</u>

You and I are on a wooden porch;
It is late spring and my legs are draped
Lazily over your lap.

The windows of our house are wide

Open.

The house breathes like a baby
Asleep.

Your left hand absently
Rubs my knee
While we smile
In contented silence
Watching children
Playing on our street.

<u>February Fifth in the Library</u>

Is this moment the result of mutual infatuation
Or merely a fevered dream of my restless imagination,
Weaving wedding veils from vows unspoken
And love unrequited?

Had you even intended the subtext in your proposal?
You proposed an oblique coupling in a context
Far in the future.

Of course, I
Accepted.

The intangible

I.

I excel in the intangible;
Those things unable to be touched
And unable to be seen,
Although they are felt,
Perceived.

II.

I love my love
As sunlight loves
The winding stream:
Attending but never touching.
I love my love
As embers of a controlled flame:
Remaining constant,
However stagnant,
Watching time carry
All else
Onward.

<u>Light</u>

I am afraid of
Him.
Not in the way I
Was afraid of the one
Before,
And his anger
Like fire burning beneath
Cool darkness.
No, I am afraid of
This one
Because of his light.
It radiates with
Strength,
A golden purity I
Have never before witnessed.

<u>Wildfire</u>

We are flames seeking sensation
Groping in the shadows we created.
We are insatiable in our cravings
For greatness.
Each breath is heat and wind
As we become more wild.

Free me of convention,
Make my love reckless and
My life bold.

Sestina: Production of a Show

Young limbs form lines like shadows,
cast from naked trees in the crisp part of winter afternoons,
on splintered wood platforms where we have lain
waiting for dreams to visit.
in vain we waste our waning hours
searching for a pleasant definition of oblivion.

We sleep lovesick with eyes wide open, oblivion
in our reach just beyond the shadows
of the lives we pursue. For hours
we dream away our youthful afternoons
allowing life's absolutes visit
without worry. We remain content where we have lain.

Clothes now strewn and lain
over the dark edges of stage we know as oblivion
we see our lives are but a brief visit
to spotlight and smoke and soft shadows
which make even the brightest, palest afternoons
fill our eyes with deep saturation of color--obscure the hour--

Weeks pass as centuries and our hour
we awaken from the dark places where we have lain
as one explosion of light which blinds the afternoons
and exposes sight to the edges of oblivion
which we redefine as light melts into shadows
And chaos makes its entrance to visit

But we welcome it. Each visit

with disaster brings us closer; we breathe as one for the fleeting
hour
we are alive and animate. One body casting one shadow
One empty stage gaping where we have lain
One empty stage greeting oblivion
We banish the light of afternoons.

Afternoons
Bleed into the most innocent visit
with divinity, with the numb ecstasy of oblivion.
The sand which spills to seal our hour
now flows freely to fill emptiness where we have lain.
We, and all which lies beyond us, melt into unified shadow.

We bid goodbye to our hour
body bids goodbye to the niche where we have lain
We dissolve with light, splintered wood, sand, and empty stage.
Into shadow.

<u>A Letter: To define the Way in Which I Love You</u>

To define the way in which I love you would never capture it truthfully. The eclipsing totality of the way in which I love you transcends the fumbling awkwardness of word or phrase. To define the way in which I love you would be to betray these years of love and amity in favor of a word--a fleeting phrase of sycophantish syllabic stress.

That is both too much and not enough.

For you are more than a definition; you are a manner of thought and feeling exemplified in human form. To attribute cliches to your name and mien would be to generalize or misrepresent you. You are not, to me, a passionate attraction nor an ephemeral amity. You and I are a connection, soul to soul, without the friction of flesh. Platonic love describes, in the nearest accuracy, our years of shared existence, though it still falls short of holistic truth.

To define the way in which I love you with lacy words would not represent your character, and puritanical bluntness would not represent my feelings. To define the way in which I love you is unnecessary--all that matters is that I love you.

Your friend,

Iris

<u>Triolet</u>

I watch time tear away my treasures,
Replacing songs my heart calls home
With foreign notes in sprawling measures.
I watch time tear away my treasures--
My dearest, simplest, childhood pleasures--
are faded, distant, near unknown
I watch time tear away my treasures,
Replacing songs I've sung since youth.

<u>On Love</u>

Is this love?
I am lost in the sweet hazel
Of his eyes,
In the crinkles
Of his smile,
The warm touch
Of his hand.

I am victim
And perpetrator
Of heartbreak.
I am the sinner
And the saved.
We must sacrifice
To love and
To be loved.
However I have suffered
Nothing.

I fear his kindness.
His apparent perfection
The way light radiates from within him
And attempts to banish pain.

But in favor of what?
In the absence of pain
There is no joy.
In the absence of suffering
There is no love.

<u>Butterfly Flight</u>

I watched the way
A butterfly flies:
Wildly beating, then
Gliding,
Dancing on the wind
Just breaths away
From its lover.

What an erratic way to love,
Tremulous and fainting then
Releasing control,
Fighting gravity only
To succumb to it.

And the days seem to scatter
like handfuls of tossed glitter
around the once-lively park.

I walk in solitude
to catch the memories
In greedy, glimmering fistfuls;
All the innocent triumphs of life seem to spin and change,
Reflecting impassioned flashes of molten sunset,
As they float to the grass underfoot,
Carried on the sighing breath of summer wind.

I run to collect the years like treasures
Armful after armful like a
Child,
and guard them till they escape,
till they slip out of my clutching fingertips
Carried away
To some other place.

Chess

It began innocently enough:
He wanted
To teach me
Chess.
He said he had played it
Growing up
With his father.

I would be good at it
Because I was smart.

I learned the basics and played
Exclusively
With him.

He laughed because
I was not good at it;
At least, not good
Compared to
Him.

I could evade capture for
Long enough,
Defending until my king was exposed.
He knew my weaknesses.

We played chess
For months,
In stagnant, stuffy library rooms
My cheeks growing hot with

Embarrassment
As he chuckled and won
Again.

I was dumb,
Or at least,
Not as smart as
Him.

But I was getting better.

Not at chess,
But at learning my place.

<u>A Dream of Adolescence (2014)</u>

"I had the strangest
Dream last night,
Which lingers in my mind,
To haunt my heart
And tease my soul
In waking hours of day."

"What is this dream,
This phantom thought,
That lingers, still, my dear?
Tell me,
Let dreams be words on freeing wings,
To reach my bending ear."

"There was a place
I cannot name,
With someone I do know--
But in my dream
He
Loved me--
Which I know not to be true.
He held me with
Good news and joy
Pouring from his gentle lips.

A-flutter,
I,
Surprised by love
Once only felt in secret
Awoke,

With rose painted
About my cheek,
And smile playing on
My lips.

There was a place
I cannot name,
With someone I do know.
But in my dream
You
Loved me.
Which I know not
To be true."

<u>If You Were Mine</u>

<u>I.</u>
Why I would clutch
The stars,
Pick them from the sky,
And make a ring
As bright as
The Milky Way.
I would swim
In the rain and music
Of a summer night,
And leave the grass
Star diamond dusted,
Like a trail of
pixie dust.

Why I would wear
A dress
Of blush-pink summer dawn,
And make a crown
Of pearly dewdrops
Set deep in chocolate hair.
I would waltz
In sun-filtered forests,
And send my heart in song
Over the gold green
Leafy treetops,
Like a lazy, flowing
Wind.

<u>II.</u>

If I could touch each memory
That floated from the banks of reminiscence,
I would rest them in
The palm of my pale hand.
I would watch their colors swirl on the surface,
Shining,
With the playful iridescence of a child's bubble,
And release them
To an infinite sky.

Each laugh would soon become a star,
Set into an open, silky night,
Each tear would become a pebble
On the sun and time-worn road.
Each test of faith
That I've endured,
Would shelter me as a tree.

Parallel Lines

Somewhere between delirium and depravity of sleep and love
you appear
With murky visibility, obscurity veiling your dark face.
Discrepancy confounds the pieces of me which seeks
simplicity
The murmuring silence of a Saturday night drowns the sound
of reason,
Manifesting as the distant synchronized beat of two hearts.

Somewhere on the precipice of transformation I appear.
The world before me, yet unseen, calls for me with haste and
reckless joy,
But I hesitate to move.
Where I am now, I see you,
Or the hollow form you sport,
With inky shades like shadows camouflaging your heart
Slowly breaking.
Where I am now, I am content to be--on an untouchable level
of sameness--
But uncertainty begs my eyes to shed their sight.
I close my eyes but still they save the image I have painted of
you.
You are black typewriter print staining my unseen eyelids.

Somewhere between insanity and possibility we stand now;
A countdown echoes mechanically in the distance.
Your arms do not reach for me, your voice remains vague and
inaudible;
My face is numbed to a point I can only call blankness.
Obscurity is my cloak as I walk the line parallel to you.

Uncertain if we are ever meant to meet, I wander on,
Dizzy and alone trying to find a point.
I believe I passed it long ago…

I retreat into anonymity--
I create a fortress of perfumed chemical clouds and novocaine
smiles.
Somewhere between us, chaos chose to fall.
Somewhere between a fairytale and nevermore we meet again.
Or not.

<u>Shooting Star:</u>

I.
I remember that night:
The April night masqueraded as summer.
The four of us
Sat in the stillness of the campus
That sprawled in every direction.
The fountain kept the silence from invading
The spaces between
My expressions of grief.

I grieved for my sister's loss,
The destruction it left in its wake.
I grieved for the innocence we all lost at the funeral.
I grieved for love unspoken and love unrealized.
I grieved for the realization that life is not infinite.

I grieved for my mother,
Who in the name of love
Suffered all,
For years, extinguishing burns with tears hidden behind the
steering wheel
Of a sky-blue minivan.

I grieved for the girl who had been broken
And endured in the name of time's infinity--
Who fell in love
And found light,
To find that light was fire,
Blinding and suffocating.

I grieved for love
As I watched it become perverted.
As I watched it consume,
Insatiable,
Angry,
Empty.

You all listened,
While I questioned the existence
Of love that will not burn us
Of love that will not melt our realities,
Of love that will not blind.

While we reflected,
We turned our eyes to the smooth, unmoving satin sky
And watched
As a shooting star crossed the horizon,

Its light cool, and white as water.

It would appear
That no amount of poetry
Can cleanse me of this tainted feeling--
This numbness which pervades throughout my soul
On clouded days and nights when I seek sensation.

Neither the scent of flowing water,
Nor that of purple impatiens,
Nor the color of deep summer storms,
Can move me.
Though I feel the cool stone beneath my bare feet
It does not truly reach me.
The calluses on my heels
Dull the world which touches me.
My body suffocates beneath the linen
Clinging desperately around it,
Begging for purpose.

If I could once more be free,
To embrace the world and all its breezes,
All its rivers and all its stones,
All its small and adoring creatures,
Baring all my skin,
Feeling the glory of worldly sensation
Regardless of the clouds,
Why I would weep.
I would crumble into pebbles to be smoothed by the bright
fountain,
And become poetic.

<u>Dandelions/Wish Flowers</u>

In your youth,
You are the picture of rebellious vibrancy,
Your thick golden petals
Bursting forth
As infant suns planted
In suburban grass
And untouched prairie fields.

In your old age,
You are hope to the youth.
Your presence
Attracts others like you,
With your wild, grey mane
And reckless propagation of wishes.

<u>Paralysis</u>

The soft give of the earth
Beneath my feet
Reminds me of
The transformative nature of the world.
Each moment, supple ground gives way beneath
The feet of some strange traveler.

Blades of grass are consumed, and
Leaves are uprooted by an impartial, sighing wind.
When I am paralyzed by the confines of my mind
And my linear conception of time and matter: the world
In relation to
Me,

I break from fear and breathe,
Remembering the soft forgiveness of this soil
And of my human skin.
I pause and remember
The transience of wet mud on skin,
When faced with clear water,
And the parallel movement of my hair
To blades of grass, or leaves in the breeze.
I remember the give of my own flesh beneath soft pressure
And the fear disappears,

Like wet mud on flesh.

<u>A Vignette for Grief of Time's Passing</u>

I still remember walking side by side in the dark, sleepy coolness of the winter night air. Around us, a sea of empty cars broken up by beacons, streetlights. We were smiling after a long night inside, avoiding the pulsing crowds of young bodies radiating reckless fire and feigned freedom.

This was an intimate moment.

Without the greed of flesh, without the need for more, we walked.

You gave me your jacket to keep me warm without my asking.

You always knew how to love me.

<u>A Letter to a Ghost</u>

I still grieve you.

I see your face when I least expect it, bursting forth from the currents of my memory in overpowering waves. I see your eyes and your hair; I see the honesty you hid from me in those helpless, child's eyes. I see the way your face cracked into a laugh when we spoke. I see the days you were kind to me.

I hear your voice when I am alone. I hear it in the way I still phrase things, years later. I hear it in the voices of my friends when we talk about things you liked.

I feel the intensity of our love. I feel overcome by your passions, overcome by your demons. I feel the longing I felt sitting in an island of light among darkness, just close enough to you to feel your gravity.

I still grieve your loss. We could have been beautiful. I could have helped you. I certainly loved you, despite my efforts to deny that fact. There will be a part of me that never stops loving you, I think. You changed me.

I still remember our first date in a playground after dark. You wore a leather jacket and made a fool of yourself trying to impress me. You spoke in circles and twisted my heart around.

I remember how you found me again years later for our second first date.

I felt elated with you. My hand in yours made sense, and your company was exhilarating. You made everything more intense.

I will always grieve you for these memories. You will always haunt me as the one I couldn't save. These are irrefutable.

<u>I Bear Your Scars</u>

Scars that are not mine.
Scars resultant of your reluctance
Scars resultant of your impatience
Scars resultant of your own inability
To produce love and light after surviving your own storms.

I bear your scars

Scorched
Onto my once-virgin flesh.
When you saw that you could not feel
The Love and Light you so deeply desired to be
And settled on destruction.

You promised me protection
You promised me a respite
From the encroaching barrage of demons that haunted my
spirit.
You promised me warmth
You promised me light
But returned only the bitter words
you'd heard on the wind in your loneliness.

I bear your scars
And I always will.

I denounce your name
I cleanse your presence from my life
I say that you are nothing.

But that is a lie.

The marks you've left on my spirit
The marks you've left
In the deepest recesses of my mind
Will never fully heal.
You will never be nothing.

You will haunt me in my dreams until my last breath.
Your ghost will appear when I least expect it
In an old set of clothes,
In a set of eyes much younger than your own,
In the cutting words of a mouth just as bitter as your own.

I wonder on these days,
In these moments of grey-blue solitude
Where Time sears new life into dead scar tissue,
If you are satisfied.

I wonder if you intended this torture.
I wonder if you are tortured, too,
By the voices and the wind that caused your callousness.
I wonder if you see me in your dreams,
A victim of your inability to love and thrive
As tempered flame and humankind have loved.
I wonder if you have sealed those wounds
That opened wide your mouth in anger,
That opened wide your mind in twisting lies,
That wounded me.

I will always bear your scars,
Try as I might to escape.

On grey-blue misty days
After beautiful respites away from thoughts of you,
I can always count on your return:

the searing of my heart
With a burn so hot it chills me,
And I am engulfed
With the snow of ashes
And memories
That my flesh and soul cannot withstand.

The Pen Excalibur

When you and I became an
"Us"
It was winter of our eighth grade year.
On the last day of school
You gave me a gift,
Carefully wrapped,
For me to open at home.

In my daffodil-walled bedroom,
I shut the door and opened this gift.

Inside were a plush, blue pleather journal
Secrets held together by a magnetic strap,
Embossed with flowers,
And a silver Sharpie pen.

I was elated.
Our mutual love of writing and poetry,
Your care and understanding of me,
Were solidified in that moment.

A decade later and we've long since parted.
I no longer dream of your faded milkshake hair
Or the brilliant, resonant rumble of your voice.
I no longer see your smile in my mind
Or reminisce on the days you swore you'd marry me someday.

But out of this comes
A moment

Like the current or tide of some long dried-up lake,
These memories come flooding back to me,
In the office supply aisle of a store in a town
Hundreds of miles away from where you and I fell
In love.

In a plastic case, on the top shelf,
Glinting in the fluorescent light
Which perpetuates the illusion of daylight, there sits,
That pen.
That silver pen,
Like Excalibur in the hands of
A Lady like Fate.

I smile as I am transported back
To summer runs in the golden sunlit park by your house.
To our middle school graduation sitting side by side,
Your speech and my poetry representing our class.

I wonder where you are now,
And whether you are still writing.

I wonder whether you, too,
Have moments like these in which
I visit you
Like an apparition
Or a dream.

I wonder if these visits are kind,
Kind as you the winter of our eighth grade year.

<u>Fir Tree (Rework 2013)</u>

Fir tree, shielding my eyes
from the gray and endless world around me
shielding me from the blurring fog of bustle and of numbness.

Fir tree, arms spread o'er me
shielding me from pouring rain
from the quiet tears of the dead.

Fir tree, shielding me
from the cutting wind
from the heartache that may come my way.

Someday the world may change
and I will be here waiting til then,
waiting, afraid
beneath this fir tree.

<u>Children</u>

They try to imitate
Adults,
"Maturity",
And find that it is
Destruction.
They crash like atoms
(the existence of which
They are yet ignorant)
Leaving broken hearts and
Broken bodies,
Littered like birthday party confetti
Around them.

They play pretend
Acting sorrow
Until it becomes real.
They mime sex and love
Until the incongruence of
Their bodies
And deeds
Forces
Equilibrium.

I, in my old and wizened age,
Stand witness to their rapture,
Their triumph, their disaster.
I, in my old age,
Imitate jeunesse
Draped in brilliant colors,
Patterns that hide

The cracks, wrinkles, and scars
On my skin.
I play pretend and search
For the days when
I was someone.
When I
Could be
Someone.

Stripped of all that could have been,
However,
I am left with what is.

What is
Is hollow.
What is
Is a dead man's float,
Having achieved that which I'd set out to do,
And wanting for joy and meaning in it.
What is
Is stagnancy,
A marsh in which I am alone,
Watching streams in their swiftness to change,
Watching clouds in their buoyancy and hope,
Watching all else progress and grow in their age.

I am a cautionary tale,
Hollow omen.
I am like the tree,
Broken bark,
Vacant core,
Searching for purpose

Since life in its truest sense
Has left me.

I am a momentary refuge,
For the youth
Riveted
By the ills
Of their misbegotten
Maturity.
I make my emptiness
Into a home,
My songs
A lighthouse.

I pray that they will rest in me a while,
Unburden themselves of secret pain;
Bequeath it unto me.

I pray that I may give them joy,
And hope,
And love like
A mother.
I pray that through my pain,
I pray that through my strife,
I pray that through my numbness,
That I may be a vessel for
Joy,
Hope,
Peace,
Celebration.

<u>On a Morning In April</u>

I awake
To the rosy blush
Of dawn
Out my window.
Rose petals set into a powder blue, slate sky.

I awake to the sweet haze
Of morning
Still curling around the trees,
Obscuring the sharp edges of cars and homes,
Still brushing the grass with dew, absently.

I awake to the sweet song
Of birds
Nature's bells ringing in
The glory,
The promise,
 of another day.

The sun glows
Molten glass
On the horizon
In fiery apple red
In juicy peach pink
And citrus orange.

Blueish light filters in
The windows of my house,
Washing the white walls with softness,
Highlighting curve and shadow.

From my nest
In the sky
I rest in awe
Of Life.
Of spring,
Of God.
Of all of creation
And its unique malleability.

I am grateful for the softness
Of my body,
My pale beige skin
And the dimpling of my fat
On bone.

I am grateful
That my face blushes
With the same radiating florals
As the morning sky in April.

I am grateful
That my hair and eyes
Reflect the colors of the earth and stone.

I am grateful
For my place
Here, on Earth,
As long as it may last.

<u>A Sticky Afternoon in May</u>

My desk is a mess.
I sit slumped over, elbows on worn hardwood, that is
Somehow warped, dull, shining, and strong
All at once.

Bullshit self help books,
Void of my own written efforts,
Decorate the corners of it.

A broken violin bow looms
Behind me,
Horse hair splayed
And limp,
Fraying frantically
And helplessly
Under the stage lights.

Unraveling,
Like my mind.
Like the pocket of a sixth grader's jacket
Which she cut open with the art teacher's scissors
After a field trip.

My mind,
Which sits and rolls between
My ears,
Like a ball of shit rolled by a shelled beetle.
Thoughts indistinct, inert, &
Fizzing like a bath bomb in
A warm tub.

Like a goldfish floating
Belly up.

It's mid-May
And the lifeblood
Of the school is draining
Quickly.
Spilling
Spilling
Down the drain;
Time and tears consume all
Indiscriminately.
The voracious hunger
Of emptiness
Makes gluttons of us all
As the end approaches.

My desk is a mess, and
I'm running out of time.

<u>Midwestern Escapism</u>

I'd like to lie in one of those fields
On the side of the highway,
Far away from everything
I've ever known and
Everything
I'll ever know.

I'd like to bask in that unknowing,
In the golden grace of evening
Among the corn and wildflowers,
Weeds and wild things.

<u>Hellfire</u>

I will take this anger
And harness it as hellfire,
And rain it down upon you
To burn
To melt,
To detonate
Everything you've ever loved.

Since my love was not adequate,
Since the fires in which we were forged
Are the fires that now break us,
I will let go of the past,
I will let go of any mercy,
And embrace destruction.

<u>For Kayla</u>

When we were teenagers,
And freedom was intoxicating,
We crashed into each other like atoms:
Reckless and radiating promise,
Dreaming of brilliance,

That's when I met you.

When we were teenagers,
Too bold and resilient to acknowledge
The effects of each collision of hearts
That occurred in the blinding stage lights
Or placid darkness of tour buses steadily coursing
Over highways pulsing with headlights,

We feel together

With the unwavering intent of burning brightly
In the most vivid of supernovas
Together.

We wove tapestries of beautiful, reckless fantasies:
Making music enveloped in the cavernous intimacy of a
concert hall
Soaring over highways to explore ourselves as well as this
Earth,
Creating torrents of laughter as we tore through rain, hand in
hand,

We burned brightly.

We did what we set out to do,
And four years passed in a dizzying euphoria
Of feigned adulthood and spontaneity.

We burned brightly,
And now we float

In the fragments of stars
And newborn galaxies
Created from the rubble of our hearts.

We float
Into the constant, burning light
Of the future,
And dream

Of when
We were teenagers.

<u>To Be A Tree</u>

To be a tree
In its rapture;
Naked body bared
And stretched
Against glinting sunlight and sighing and at the birth of spring,
Arms stretched upward
In exultation.

To be a tree
In its fervor
Casting leaf and limb aside
Sacrificing self for
Oneness
With torrential gale and
Dancing earth.

To be a tree
In its maternity
Housing fauna, flora, fungus,
Becoming a rainbow of her own,
Protecting all her kith and kin.

To be a tree
In its infancy
Supple sapling
Digging roots down deep
Nourished by the loam, silt, clay.
Holding on, swinging, praying,
In awe of that which grows around it.

The Ocean

When I think about the ocean,
I think of the color green--
The deep, ethereal, emerald green of the cliffs of Moher
That fringed the sea.

49

I think of being sixteen
And still in love with you,
Tall like a sturdy tree,
Warm like home,
With rusty hair like fire.

The ebb and flow
Of our affections
And opportunities
Never seemed to line up.

So my lasting memories of you
Are of the ocean,
The cliffs of Moher,
Of Kilarney,
And at their core,
Of a boy in a green sweatshirt
Towering, arms around me.

<u>Roots</u>

Being dependent upon
That which thrives in darkness,
Away from the light
Of love
Of truth,
Gaining strength
From the tears of God,
It is a natural consequence
That the fruit
May sour and spoil.

Being taught from a young age
"You are nothing without me",
With the only option of escape being
A great plunge from heaven
To earth,
Ensuring certain death,
It only follows that
Life
Would be
Short
And
Bitter.

Teacher of self-loathing,
Teacher of anger and fear,
You have shown me
The antithesis
Of love.

I pray that I
Never grow
To be like
You.

<u>Duplicity</u>
> *I.   Love*

You have
Me.

You have all of me:
Mind, body, and heart.
The softness Of
Your flesh on mine,
The sweetness of
Your voice in my ear,
The serendipity of
Your love
Given to me.

The fruit of our journey
Together
Is sweet.
Nectar from the young, sweet flower
Of spring.

> *II.   Deceit*

You have
Broken me.

You have broken
My very definition
Of love

With your careless
Duplicity.

Every fear
Every demon
You had banished
With the pure flame
Of your love
Returns
With the discovery
That none of this
Was real.

Your plainness,
Your meanness,
Your lies,
Have tainted
The sanctity of
Our home,
Have spoiled the fruits
Of the garden.

All that was crumbles
To ash.
As I am ripped
From my eden.

I stand
Alone
In the wreckage
Of our love:
Suffocating smoke,

Embers extinguishing
As they fall
Into a crush
In my hair.

<u>Friendship</u>

I do the dishes
In your kitchen,
You build a bed
By the window.
In this silence,
Busy silence
I feel at peace
For the first time
In a long time.

And I think I'd be content
To stay with you here
For all my life
Within this shimmering, waking dream.

You lean your head
On my shoulder,
We sit, tired, on your couch.
In this moment,
Precious moment
I become aware
That we are meant
To be together
Like this,
For all
Of this life
And whatever adventure
It may bring.

<u>Soul Mate</u>

"I will find you
In this life,
And every life".

"I choose you,
I will always
Choose you."

<u>Confession</u>

Confession defined:
The blessed sacrament,
Which must be completed before
Communion, before
Marriage.

The reality of Confession:
There is nothing blessed,
Nothing holy,
About the heartbreak and rage
I feel
Upon receiving your words.

I refuse
To absolve you of your sin.

All things end,
Whether violently or
Peacefully.

All change
Implies pain
To some extent:
Metamorphosis requires
The sacrifice of what was
In favor of a beautiful future.

I pray that this end
Creates galaxies
Full of life,
And stars
That will be wished upon
By children
For ages onward.

I pray that the legacy
The result
Of this explosion
Will have more meaning
Than it appears to
At this time.

I set myself ablaze
Gasoline and tears
Dancing in the fields
Next to the highway.

In front of me
A granary
Of some small town
With no name,
No people.

And a horizon
As far as the eye can see.

I feel the ecstasy of
The sun,
As she burns
For those who scorn
And shun
Her.

I feel the rapture
Of the tree outstretched,
The cool touch
Of the ever-shifting soil
Underfoot
As it singes.

I am
Living star,
Let them see my light,
Let him feel
My heat.